Chain REACTION

By Mike Dion
Illustrated by DJ Simison

West Jackson
Intermediate School

Celebration Press
Pearson Learning Group

Contents

CHAPTER 1

The Before-School Crisis

Sophie Lenski reached for her backpack. It was almost time to catch the bus, but she didn't feel ready for school. Mr. Naylor wanted everyone to bring in an idea for a science project that a team could do. Sophie didn't have one. She was so deep in thought she barely heard her little brother, Gabe.

"Sophie!" he said. "Help me look! I can't find them!"

Gabe was in second grade. Every single school day he lost something—or forgot something.

Sophie's big sister Rachel breezed into the kitchen.

"You can't find something?" she teased. "So what else is new!"

Rachel was in sixth grade. She was smart and funny, and she talked almost as much as Gabe did.

"Sophie!" begged Gabe.

"She's off in La-La Land," said Rachel. "Earth to Sophie! You're daydreaming!"

"I'm worrying," said Sophie, "not daydreaming."

Everyone in the fourth and fifth grades had to do team projects for the science fair. Mr. Naylor's class always won a prize— they were famous for it.

Sophie wasn't great at science, and she was used to doing things alone. But she hoped to be part of a winning team. Also she wanted her teammates to be glad she was one of them. What could she contribute?

"Sophie!" wailed Gabe. He had eyes like spotlights and beamed them at Sophie.

"What did you lose?" she asked.

"My library books! They're due today, and I can't find them!"

"You'd better find them, Gabe," said Rachel. "In two minutes we leave for the bus stop."

Gabe's expression became tragic. "They'll never let me take out any more books!" he wailed.

"Go look in your room," directed Rachel.

Dad and Mom both left for work a few minutes before the school bus arrived, so Rachel was in charge of getting Gabe to the bus stop. It was not an easy job.

Gabe moaned and stomped down the hall. "I can't find them!" he called as soon as he reached the door to his room.

"I'll help you look," sighed Rachel.

Sophie swung her backpack over her right shoulder. She leaned as far sideways as she could and tried to hook her left arm through the left strap. Getting her backpack on was always a struggle. She could ask Rachel for help, but she preferred to do things herself.

The sounds of Rachel's Mom-voice and Gabe's help-me voice came down the hall, and Sophie grinned. Gabe was a handful, but he was fun. She glanced at his backpack. Gabe liked to pretend his backpack was a parachute, and he could get it on in two seconds.

Sophie paused a moment. Parachutes— maybe she could suggest a science project about parachutes?

On the third try Sophie got her left arm through the strap. She settled her backpack between her shoulders as Rachel pulled Gabe down the hall.

"We don't have any more time to look," Rachel scolded. "Next time take better care of your books!"

Gabe was wearing his full-of-woe face. "Poor guy," thought Sophie. She picked up his backpack and handed it over.

Gabe's face lit with hope. "My books!" he cried.

He grabbed the backpack and peered in. "No books," he groaned. "And one was awesome—all about tree frogs!"

"Maybe the frogs hopped away," teased Rachel.

Gabe moaned. He had no sense of humor when he was upset. Now Sophie thought they really might miss the bus, but she was always the last one in her family to give up on anything. She decided to help Gabe "take a walk backward through his mind"—a way to remember that almost always worked.

"Gabe had some library books," she began. "First he brought them . . . into the house. Next he brought them . . . ."

Gabe screwed up his face comically, thinking hard.

"We don't have time for this now," warned Rachel.

Sophie glanced out the window while she waited for Gabe to name what happened next. She spotted the school bus at the corner. She turned to her brother. "Come on, Gabe," she cheered him on silently.

Gabe's face cleared. "Next I brought the books into the playroom!" he cried.

"Next he put them . . . ," Sophie prompted.

"Down by the fish tank!" shouted Gabe triumphantly. He bolted down to the playroom.

Sophie heard Gabe's muffled "Got 'em!" as she headed out to meet the bus. Then her mind drifted back to her own problem— what to suggest as a team science project. Sophie sighed. She wished she could solve her own problems as easily as she was able to help Gabe solve his!

CHAPTER 2

Team Two

Sophie was the third student to reach Mr. Naylor's classroom. It was her own secret race each day, and her speed showed improvement. She liked to say her leg brace didn't slow her down; it just gave her a different way of walking. She never reached the classroom first, though—not yet anyway.

"Let's get settled down quickly," Mr. Naylor advised. "Then we can meet with our science project teammates before music class."

Would Sophie's teammates be kids she could work with? She already knew one of her teammates—Margo Inman.

She and Margo had already asked if they could work together. Mr. Naylor said yes, but he wouldn't let them choose the rest of their team.

Sophie flashed Margo a smile. They were about to find out who their teammates would be.

Mr. Naylor called the class to order. "For our science projects our class will have five teams," he said. "Notice that each table is numbered, from one to five. When you hear your name and team number, please move to your team table."

Mr. Naylor began to read from his list. With groans and laughter the four members of Team One moved to their table.

"Stuart Salter and Howard Wade," read Mr. Naylor. "Team Two."

"Wow, that's some pair!" thought Sophie. Stuart was so shy he never said a word, and Howard Wade talked so much no one else ever got a word in edgewise.

"Also Sophie Lenski and Margo Inman," continued Mr. Naylor. "Team Two."

Sophie and Margo gaped at each other.

"Do we have to?" whispered Margo.

Sophie knew they had to. She followed Margo to the table that Howard and Stuart already shared. She pulled out a chair and tried to smile. She'd never said more than two words to either Stuart or Howard. She hardly knew them! How could their team win with the four of them on it?

Mr. Naylor finished calling teams. Team Two avoided looking at one another. After Mr. Naylor said for the teams to trade ideas and decide on a project, Margo took over.

"Okay, Team Two," she said briskly. "What kind of team project would you guys be interested in doing?"

Stuart shrugged. Howard leaned his elbows on the table and bounced on one leg. This was a team? Sophie felt she ought to suggest something.

"How about parachutes?" she asked.

"Yeah, parachutes!" cried Howard. "Parachutes that don't open, so SPLAT! Or we could do car wrecks. You know, what happens to cars when they crash? Do they flip over or crunch or explode?"

"Explode?" repeated Margo in her let-me-get-this-straight voice.

"Yeah!" said Howard. He stood up and waved his arms. "We can do explosions!"

"Explosions aren't practical," said Margo. "Think about it."

Howard was so eager that Margo's protest didn't bother him.

"Then let's do volcanoes!" he exclaimed. "Volcanoes explode naturally!"

Mr. Naylor came up behind Howard's chair and listened for a moment.

"Didn't you do a volcano for your science project last year, Howard?" he asked.

Howard nodded. "Last year my volcano was better than my second-grade volcano!" he exclaimed. "With four of us we can make a really huge one!"

Sophie felt like a kettle about to steam. If they were going to build a volcano, they might as well do a science project with her brother, Gabe! Team Two needed a better project than that to win a prize!

"I don't want to do a volcano," she protested.

"Oh, come on!" said Howard.

"I think you'll need to move beyond volcanoes this year, Howard," said Mr. Naylor. "It's time to apply that imaginative mind of yours to another project."

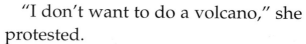

Gabe
Lily
Sarah
Sully

PG17

"Rats," said Howard. He slumped over the table. Mr. Naylor moved on, and Margo turned to Stuart.

"What interests you, Stuart?" she asked.

Stuart shrugged. "Animals, I guess," he said.

Howard stood up. "Animals!" he said. "Instead of volcanoes?"

He started talking about famous volcanoes of the world and how molten rock can erupt from volcanoes. Sophie had to admire him. He certainly knew a lot about his subject! Margo tried to regain control of the team meeting.

"What was your parachute idea, Sophie?" she asked.

"I didn't really have an exact idea," said Sophie, "except maybe something about how some seeds are like parachutes . . . ."

But neither Howard nor Stuart was listening. Howard explained how to build great volcanoes, and Stuart doodled. Some team! Would they ever pull together?

Mr. Naylor called time, and Sophie pushed away from the table. This was even worse than what she'd imagined! The way things were going, Team Two wouldn't even have a plan, let alone win a prize!

That night Sophie gave up on her homework and played with Gabe. They built a great marble mover with Gabe's wooden marble chute blocks.

"Maybe Team Two can do something with chutes and marbles," she thought. But what?

CHAPTER 3

Teamwork?

Sophie brought a new notebook to the next science project meeting. She'd printed one word inside: *marbles*. Margo brought notes, Stuart had some drawing paper and magic markers, and Howard just brought himself.

Sophie still wished they didn't have to do team projects. If she was working alone, she could start building something right now. She looked around the table. Would the four of them work as a team today?

"Let's say our ideas now," said Margo.

"You first, Stuart," said Sophie.

She knew Stuart would rather say nothing. But he was part of the team. Sophie wanted him to know he was as important to the team as anyone else.

"I don't have an idea," said Stuart. He doodled and looked unhappy.

"Try to think of one now," urged Sophie. "Just say whatever comes into your mind."

"Uhh, cats," said Stuart. "My cat."

"Cats!" said Howard.

"Quiet, Howard," said Margo.

"I don't have to be quiet!" he replied.

"Some teamwork!" thought Sophie.

"What about your cat?" she asked Stuart.

Stuart shrugged. "She sleeps a lot," he said.

"Sleeping cats!" exclaimed Howard.

"Why cats sleep," Margo said, interrupting Howard. She wrote it down. "Now you, Howard."

"You're not in charge!" he said.

"Come on, Howard," said Sophie. "Tell us your idea."

"Yeah," said Stuart. "I had to."

"Okay, okay. I want to do something with action," said Howard. "Like pulleys!"

"I don't see why pulleys are better than cats," grumbled Stuart.

"Quiet, Stuart," said Margo.

"Pulleys are good, Howard!" said Sophie. "What would we do for the project, exactly?"

"Uhh . . . ," said Howard.

It was clear that he was stuck, too.

"I had an idea you might like," Sophie said. "How about some kind of chain reaction with marbles?"

"What would be the point?" said Margo.

"I'm not really sure," said Sophie in a hesitant voice. So much for her idea! "What did you think of, Margo?"

"How about spina bifida?" asked Margo.

Everyone looked at Sophie. Spina bifida was the name of the condition that gave Sophie her weak back and legs.

"I already know all I want to know about spina bifida," said Sophie.

Margo blushed. "I also thought about making a model of Jupiter, with moons going around," she said.

"Time's up for today!" called Mr. Naylor.

As Sophie made her way back to her place, she heard other students talk about the projects they'd decided on. Team Five was going to measure wind speeds. Team One was going to see how heat from a 100-watt light bulb affects various materials. Team Two wasn't even a working team yet. It looked like they were going to have the worst project, not the best one.

CHAPTER 4

Fish Food

"Team Two had better think of an idea for a project by tomorrow," Sophie moaned to Rachel after school.

"I think better when I doodle," responded Rachel.

"I'll try anything," said Sophie and went down to the playroom to look for her art supplies. The playroom had a TV, an old computer, shelves of puzzles and games, and a fish tank.

Sophie wished she could just stare at the fish and leave her science project problem for later. But she decided to stick with it until she came up with an idea.

Gabe was over by the tank, singing. "Flap flap, flap your fins gently round the tank! Fishily, fishily, fishily, fishily, how the fish tank stank," he sang as Sophie approached.

She saw him drop something into the tank. Not fish food. Now what?

She watched some kind of crumb fall through the water, but not fast. It sort of swayed down.

"What did you put in the tank, Gabe?" she asked.

"Nothing!" said Gabe. "Just tiny pieces of tortilla chip! I was giving the fish a treat!"

Sophie thought about fish food. The thin flakes were so light that they didn't seem to count as food. But the weight of a tortilla chip crumb compared to the weight of a fish-food flake was like giving a baby a whole apple instead of a spoonful of applesauce.

"I don't know, Gabe," said Sophie. "Maybe we'd better clean out the tank."

"Because of the tortilla chip?" asked Gabe.

Sophie nodded. "Maybe they're a little too heavy for fish stomachs," she said.

Gabe's face turned white. "Oh no!" he cried. "Help me, Sophie, help me! Before it's too late!"

Sophie got out the net and helped him remove the soggy tortilla chips from the bottom of the tank. She thought of how the chips sank. The fish flakes stayed on top of the water and then drifted down slowly. Could that be part of a science project?

Sophie tried to figure something out, but she couldn't get anywhere with it. She'd have to keep working on it. Maybe her team could help her out tomorrow.

CHAPTER 5

Getting It Together
. . . Sort of

Four of the five tables in Mr. Naylor's classroom held happy, busy teams. Team Two's table was quiet. Quiet and gloomy.

"I think we should still use Stuart's cat," said Howard. "Stuart says she sleeps a lot. Maybe we could do a project about different ways to wake her up."

"Nothing wakes Muffin up," said Stuart.

"Well, why can't we make a volcano then?" asked Howard.

"No volcanoes," said Margo, "and we can't use a cat. A cat would do a different thing every time."

Team Two started arguing, except for Sophie. Gabe's marble game popped into her mind. Once you built a chute system, the marbles rolled down one of several chutes every time. What if, what if . . . .

She almost had an idea, but she needed help to picture it. Would her team be able to listen?

Sophie broke into her team's argument. "Listen," she said. "Remember how Howard wanted to do pulleys? And I wanted to do a marble thing? Maybe we can do both and build a machine or a toy with moving parts. A machine where *one* part moves because *another* part does."

"Huh?" said Stuart.

"What do you mean?" asked Margo.

"I know what Sophie means!" said Howard. "She means like bowling. You roll a ball, and the pins fall!"

"Exactly!" said Sophie. "Only it doesn't stop there! What if when the pins knocked into another ball, they made *that* ball roll?"

"But how do we build it?" asked Margo.

"That's the science-project part!" said Howard excitedly.

Sophie could see that Margo and Stuart still didn't understand. How could she make it clear? Maybe if she imagined explaining the machine to Gabe. . . .

"Yesterday I thought about how things fall through water," she said. "Some things fall straight down because they're heavy. Some things that don't weigh so much sort of circle down, and some things are so light they float on top."

"So what?" asked Stuart. He looked confused.

"It got me thinking about how things move," said Sophie. "So let's build a chain-reaction machine! Each person can be responsible for one part of the chain reaction, but all of us will have to figure out how it all goes together and what happens at the end."

Sophie could see now why being part of a team could be better than working alone.

"Maybe we could start with something like a stone tied to a string!" said Howard. "BAM! We could pull it back and let it go, and it could hit the marble!"

"Right!" said Sophie. "Next the marble would roll down a chute and . . . ."

Everyone stopped to think hard.

"Fall into a cup?" said Stuart.

"Sure!" said Sophie. "We could use a raisin cup from the cafeteria, and the little cup could be attached to a string on a pulley . . . ."

"Yeah!" cried Howard. "And when the marble goes in the cup, the weight pulls it down, which pulls something else up! But what?"

"I know!" said Sophie. "Maybe it's attached to a small plastic lid with fish food in it! We can make a fish-feeder machine!"

"The pulley would tip the fish food container just far enough . . . ," added Margo.

" . . . so it sprinkles into a goldfish bowl!" cried Howard. *"Cool!"*

"Sounds great," said Mr. Naylor. Sophie jumped. She hadn't heard him approach. "You're talking about a physics problem," he said. "When something moves, it has energy. How much depends on how fast it moves, and how much it weighs."

"Do you really think we can do this, Sophie?" asked Margo.

"Sure we can," said Sophie. "We just have to keep trying till it works."

She knew it was true because of her leg. She'd found out how to be almost as fast as Rachel. She couldn't speed the way Gabe and Rachel did, but she could speed in her own way. She just needed something to help her get started.

"So Team Two is going to build a Chain Reaction Fish Feeder," said Howard. "Sophie said we can do it, so we can!"

Sophie felt great. Maybe she did have something to contribute to her team. She'd found out something else too—working as part of a team was easier in some ways than doing things herself.

CHAPTER 6

Disaster!

Sophie decided to invite her team over on Saturday. They could build the machine in the playroom with real fish for inspiration.

After much talking and pleading and making deals with Gabe, she was supplying the chute and marble. Howard was bringing a small pulley, some string, and a stone. Stuart was in charge of goldfish. Today, though, he'd just bring an empty fish bowl. Margo would handle plastic cups and lids. Sophie's mom had supplied her glue gun, string, tape, cardboard, and other odds and ends—and a fresh batch of chocolate chip cookies. Sophie couldn't wait to get started.

By 10:15 everyone had arrived, raring to go. Howard had a soccer game at 1:00, so they really had to get it done by then. On Monday they'd demonstrate it for the class.

"Can I come in and watch?" asked Gabe, who took a dim view of having hot glue applied to his blocks. "Puh-leeze?"

"Not today, kiddo," said Sophie. "That was part of the deal, remember? This is like homework. You can't bug me when I'm doing my homework. But you get extra cookies. Okay?"

"Okay," grumbled Gabe, heading for the kitchen.

The team pulled out their supplies and arranged them on the table tennis table, which Sophie had covered with newspaper to keep glue off it.

"I think we should sketch out how this is going to look," said Margo. "What do you think, Stuart?"

"How can we do that when we don't *know* how it'll look?" asked Stuart.

"It's a plan, man!" responded Howard cheerfully.

Stuart got out his markers.

"If we have a marble going down a chute, we have to start everything higher than the fishbowl," said Margo.

"Maybe we should work backwards," said Sophie.

"Right!" said Howard. "Start with the fishbowl, which will be on the floor. Draw that first, right here," he commanded Stuart. Howard was really into it.

"Okay. Now, right at the edge, resting on the opening, will be the plastic lid of fish food," said Margo. "Draw that in, Stuart." Stuart drew.

"Cool!" said Howard. "Now we need to have a string attached to the lid so it'll tip. But the string is going to go through my pulley. The pulley has to be higher than the lid, so maybe right about here," he directed.

"Stuart, that is good work!" said Howard, admiring Stuart's pulley. Sophie smiled. They really were a team now! This was going to be fun.

Stuart smiled a shy smile. "I know what's next," he said. "The string goes from the lid through the pulley to the plastic raisin cup. But how do we tie the cup onto the string so that it's not lopsided?"

Sophie smiled. "Like a parachute!" she said. "We'll tie it to the cup in four places so it's even. Like this, see?" She added the cup to Stuart's sketch.

"Then we add the marble chute," said Margo. "But what's the pulley going to be attached to?"

"Hang on, hang on," said Howard. "I think the chute will need to be at the edge of a stool. Maybe we can use a wire coat hanger sticking out from the stool to hold the pulley. Sophie, do you have a stool and a coat hanger?"

"No problem, Howard!" smiled Sophie, getting up awkwardly and heading for a storage closet.

Howard added the stool and coat hanger to the sketch. "Then the stone on the string goes right here, on top of the bench—right behind the old marble! We'll have to attach the other end of the string to something so it will swing. That could be tricky!"

"How about a pencil between two boxes?" said Sophie, arriving with a hanger and an old stepstool from the closet. "Let me just make sure we can use this stool and see if Mom has some empty boxes."

When the drawing was declared complete, everyone was starving. Team Two decided to take a lunch break before starting on construction, so it was already 12:15 when they began putting the fish feeder together. No time to waste.

Sophie managed to attach string to the edge of the raisin cup in four places. Then she attached a long string to the cross strings and passed it to Howard.

He ran it through the pulley. Then he punched a hole in the plastic lid and tied the other end of the string to it. So far, so good.

Stuart used duct tape to attach the hanger to the stool so that the hook part stuck out to hold the pulley.

"You've got enough tape on that hanger to sink a ship!" teased Margo.

Stuart grinned. "Let's hang the pulley on and get the chute attached," he said. "It's almost time for Howard to go to his soccer game."

Setting up the chute turned out to be the hardest part. It had to lead the marble from the edge of the stool down to the plastic cup. None of the chutes were very long, so there would have to be a space between the end of the chute and the raisin cup. Finally, after some trial and error, and with the help of a stack of books and the glue gun, the chute seemed ready to go.

Howard stuck the pencil into the two cardboard boxes and tied the string around the pencil.

"Here we go," he said, as he lined the stone up behind Gabe's marble. The marble was perched at the edge of the stool near the chute, held still by a wad of soft putty.

Howard pulled back the stone and let it swing. The marble went flying—right over the chute and across the room.

"Hmmm," said Howard. "Don't worry. Sophie, we need one of those blocks with a tunnel through it to control the old marble."

They glued a block to the edge of the stool and moved the putty. Then they tried again.

BAM! The marble went through the block, down the chute, and missed the cup by a mile.

Margo adjusted the chute. BAM! This time the marble went right into the cup— and the pulley fell off the hanger.

It was 12:45. "I have to go," wailed Howard. "See you guys tomorrow! I hope you can get this thing to work fast!"

Off he went. The rest of Team Two looked at one another. "Let's try one more time," said Sophie. Stuart re-attached the pulley more securely.

BAM! The marble went through the block, down the chute, and into the cup . . . and the lid dumped all the fish food on the floor.

"This is a disaster!" said Margo. A horn honked outside. Mrs. Inman was there to pick Margo up for her piano lesson.

"One more try," said Sophie. "I think the lid needs to go on the other side of the bowl. Move it over more," she instructed Stuart. She swung the rock at the marble again.

BAM! The chute fell off the stool, and the marble disappeared under the fish tank.

"I have to go," wailed Margo. "C'mon, Stuart, we're dropping you off. Maybe we can practice Monday morning at school."

Before Sophie knew what happened, they were gone. So much for teamwork.

CHAPTER 7

A Team at Last

Sophie walked into class on Monday with the parts of the fish feeder in a big box, and feeling anxious. Stuart had the fish in a plastic bag. At least he'd remembered.

"So, Team Two," said Mr. Naylor when everyone was seated, "today's your day to present your project. Do you need some time to set up?"

"I'll say," said Howard. "Just give us a few minutes." They got to work in the science corner.

Quickly they reviewed what had gone wrong on Saturday and decided on some adjustments. Sophie and Margo adjusted the lid and the chute to avoid their earlier problems. Stuart taped everything together with extra tape. "I think we need one practice run," said Margo.

"Let's just go for it," said Howard.

Sophie agreed. "It's now or never," she breathed. "Okay, Mr. Naylor. We're ready!"

Howard pulled back the stone. Sophie placed the marble. Stuart closed his eyes.

BAM! The marble went through the block, down the chute, into the cup. The cup dropped, the lid tipped, and three hungry goldfish finally got lunch.

"Team Two rules!" Howard screamed, clapping Sophie on the shoulder. Stuart opened his eyes and grinned shyly. Margo sighed in relief.

Sophie smiled. Howard was right. They were a team, and at that moment, they definitely ruled!